BACKYARD WILDLIFE

Snails

By Margo Gates

BELLWETHER MEDIA • MINNEAPOLIS, MN

Note to Librarians, Teachers, and Parents:

Blastoff! Readers are carefully developed by literacy experts and combine standards-based content with developmentally appropriate text.

Level 1 provides the most support through repetition of high-frequency words, light text, predictable sentence patterns, and strong visual support.

Level 2 offers early readers a bit more challenge through simple sentences, increased text load, and less repetition of high-frequency words.

Level 3 advances early-fluent readers toward fluency through increased text and concept load, less reliance on visuals, longer sentences, and more literary language.

Level 4 builds reading stamina by providing more text per page, increased use of punctuation, greater variation in sentence patterns, and increasingly challenging vocabulary.

Level 5 encourages children to move from "learning to read" to "reading to learn" by providing even more text, varied writing styles, and less familiar topics.

Whichever book is right for your reader, Blastoff! Readers are the perfect books to build confidence and encourage a love of reading that will last a lifetime!

This edition first published in 2014 by Bellwether Media, Inc.

No part of this publication may be reproduced in whole or in part without written permission of the publisher. For information regarding permission, write to Bellwether Media, Inc., Attention: Permissions Department, 5357 Penn Avenue South, Minneapolis, MN 55419.

Library of Congress Cataloging-in-Publication Data

Gates, Margo.
  Snails / by Margo Gates.
    pages cm. – (Blastoff! readers. Backyard wildlife)
  Audience: Grades K to 3.
  Includes bibliographical references and index.
  Summary: "Developed by literacy experts for students in kindergarten through grade three, this book introduces snails to young readers through leveled text and related photos"– Provided by publisher.
  ISBN 978-1-60014-920-7 (hardcover : alk. paper)
  1. Snails–Juvenile literature. I. Title.
  QL430.4.G285 2014
  594'.3–dc23
                                                          2013000904

Printed in the United States of America, North Mankato, MN.

Contents

Snails are **mollusks** with shells. Some live on land. Others live in water.

Most snails
have a **foot**.
The foot pushes
a snail forward.

foot

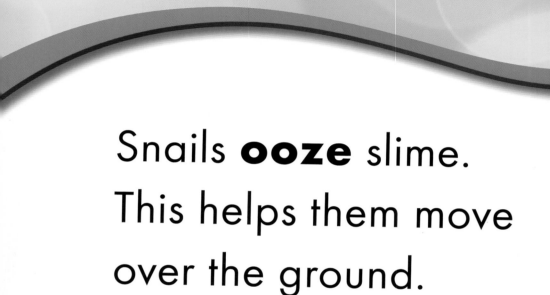

Snails **ooze** slime. This helps them move over the ground.

slime

Snails on land lay eggs in dirt. They protect the eggs with slime.

Baby snails **hatch** from the eggs. They start to eat right away.

Snails on land
eat fruits, plants,
and bark. Snails in
water eat **algae**.

algae

Snails have rows of tiny teeth. They use their teeth to **grind** food.

Snails are **prey** for snakes, frogs, and birds. They are too slow to escape these **predators**.

A snail curls up in its shell when danger is near. Then it covers the hole with its foot!

Glossary

algae—plant-like material that grows in water

foot—a long body part that spreads out under a snail's body; the foot works like a muscle to move the snail forward.

grind—to crush into smaller bits

hatch—to break out of an egg

mollusks—animals that have soft bodies and no backbones; most mollusks live in water and have shells.

ooze—to make or give off a liquid or slime

predators—animals that hunt other animals for food

prey—animals that are hunted by other animals for food

To Learn More

AT THE LIBRARY

Allen, Judy. *Are You a Snail?* New York, N.Y.:
Kingfisher, 2003.

Brown, Ruth. *Snail Trail.* New York, N.Y.:
Crown Publishers, 2010.

Waxman, Laura Hamilton. *Let's Look at Snails.*
Minneapolis, Minn.: Lerner Publications
Company, 2010.

ON THE WEB

Learning more about snails
is as easy as 1, 2, 3.

1. Go to www.factsurfer.com.

2. Enter "snails" into the search box.

3. Click the "Surf" button and you will see a
   list of related Web sites.

With factsurfer.com, finding more information
is just a click away.

Index